BEYOND
the
WILL OF GOD

CHAR KOL ESTEBAN

Beyond the Will of God

This book is written to provide information and motivation to readers. Its purpose is not to render any type of psychological, legal, or professional advice of any kind. The content is the sole opinion and expression of the author, and not necessarily that of the publisher.

Copyright © 2023 by Char Kol Esteban.

All rights reserved. No part of this book may be reproduced, transmitted, or distributed in any form by any means, including, but not limited to, recording, photocopying, or taking screenshots of parts of the book, without prior written permission from the author or the publisher. Brief quotations for noncommercial purposes, such as book reviews, permitted by Fair Use of the U.S. Copyright Law, are allowed without written permissions, as long as such quotations do not cause damage to the book's commercial value. For permissions, write to the publisher, whose address is stated below.

Printed in the United States of America.

ISBN 978-1-64552-188-4 (Paperback)
ISBN 978-1-64552-187-7 (Digital)

Lettra Press books may be ordered through booksellers or by contacting:

Lettra Press LLC
30 N Gould St. Suite 4753
Sheridan, WY 82801
1 307-200-3414 | info@lettrapress.com
www.lettrapress.com

TABLE OF CONTENTS

Introduction vii
Stolen Nightmares ix
Chapter 1   The Prophecy 1
Chapter 2   Franklin Life 3
Chapter 3   Hold Your Head Up 5
Chapter 4   Transition 7
Chapter 5   Identity Crisis 9
Chapter 6   The Road to Renee 11
Chapter 7   Introduction to Hell 13
Chapter 8   Out of the Frying Pan 17
Chapter 9   She said, "Yes, Yes, Yes" 19
Chapter 10 Scandalous 23
Chapter 11 Guess Who's Coming to Dinner? 25
Chapter 12 Possible Reasons 29
Chapter 13 March 2, 1975, 'The Day of Infamy' 33
Chapter 14 James' Monkey 35
Chapter 15 A Look at the US Air Force 39
Chapter 16 One Step Closer 45
Chapter 17 "Operator, who's been calling?" 49
Chapter 18 First Born 51
Chapter 19 God Bless this Hell 55
Chapter 20 Godsend 59
Chapter 21 Them Changes 63
Chapter 22 Renee, what are you going to do? 65
Chapter 23 Reconstruction 69
Chapter 24 Damned from the Beginning 73
Chapter 25 Petitioner or Respondent? 75
Chapter 26 Goodbye Renee 77
Chapter 27 Life after Divorce 81

INTRODUCTION

Attention Readers! In an effort to start with a similar mindset, please examine this photograph. This historical moment in our nation contributed to significant social change. The assassination of Martin Luther King, Jr. (MLK) on April 4, 1968, at the Lorraine Motel in Memphis, Tennessee. This photograph shows MLK lying on the balcony floor and members of his entourage pointing at the direction of the shooter. Would this be natural response after hearing a gun go off and seeing someone in your proximity fall with blood gushing from his head?

I have been in situations where gun shots or even the mention of someone having a gun resulted in everyone running for Cover. Self-preservation automatically kicks in. Pointing at the location of where the shots were fired is not the first response in a chaotic situation. When a can of Black Flag or Raid is sprayed on a colony of roaches, how would they respond? Are they first going to identify the location of this deadly spray, or are they going to scatter in every direction? The members of MLK's entourage appear to be calm and focused on the location of the shooter instead of running for shelter. This implies possible prior knowledge of the event. Even if I had prior knowledge and the sniper was an expert, I would still run like hell!

Another factor warranting serious scrutiny is the person who took this photograph. Was it just a coincidence that he was at the right place and time to get the perfect shot? How long did he have to wait in the bushes? Like the sniper, the photographer must have had prior knowledge of the event.

The assassin, the victim's entourage, and the photographer all appeared to have prior knowledge of the assassination. Every picture tells a story, and this picture supports a theory of a deeper involvement. MLK was perceived as a threat to the nation and had to be terminated. J. Edgar Hoover, Director of the Federal Bureau of Investigation, claimed MLK was a Public Enemy. With the degree of power coming from the top, MLK's death was not a difficult task. Who were those with prior knowledge and what did they have to gain?

STOLEN NIGHTMARES

They say that everyone has at least one story to tell. Unfortunately for me, I've got about a million. This story is about the manifestation of a prophecy and all the dynamics involved. It is not intended to place judgement, but to give an accurate and objective assessment of the events discussed.

People are always saying that things happen for a reason. Of course, they do! If I drive though a red light and have an accident, the reason for the accident is obvious. Things don't just happen out of a vacuum. There is always a root cause. That root cause could be traced back through generations. I'm sure, if I researched deep enough, I could obtain a better understanding why things happen in my life.

In order to prevent going off the deep end into infinity, I will narrow this story to pertain to events I've experienced in this physical life.

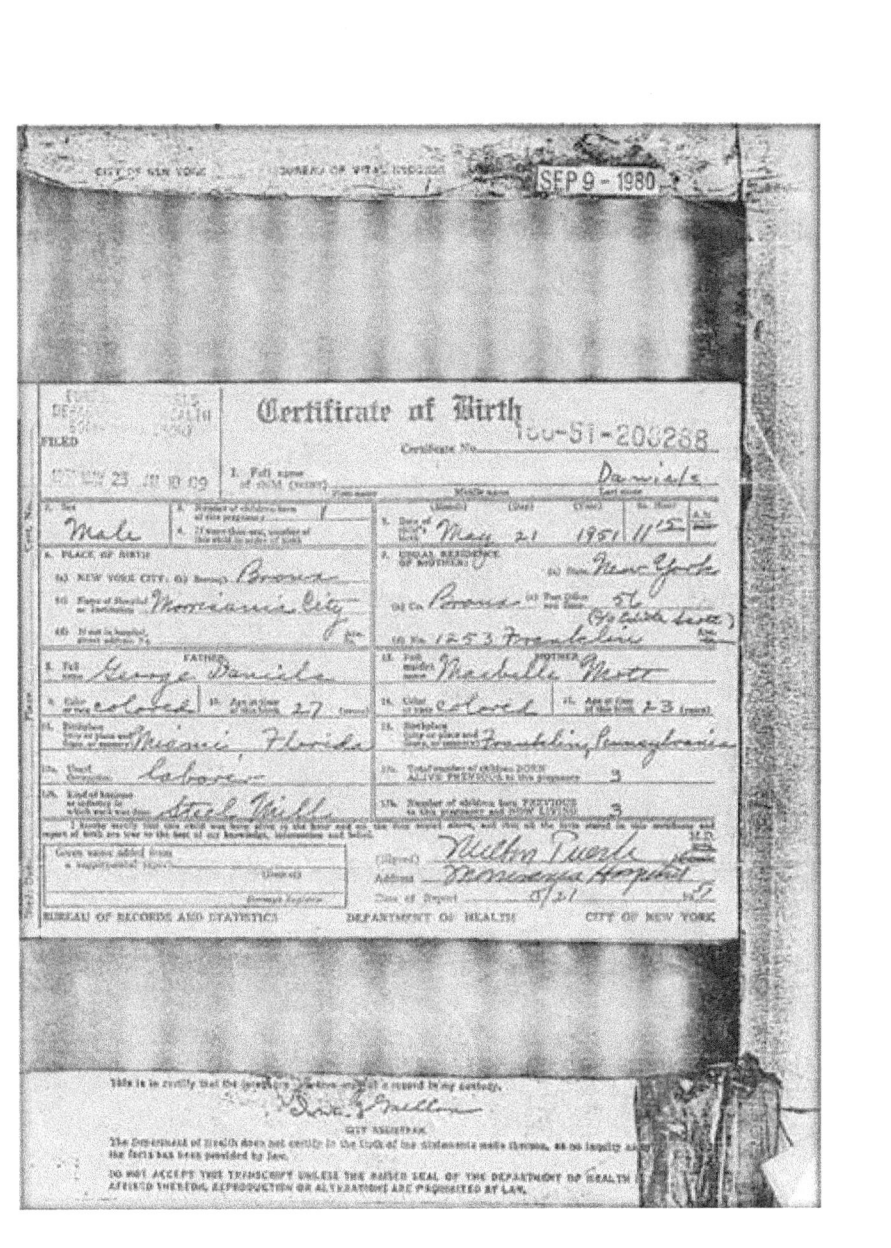

CHAPTER ONE

The Prophecy

As far back as I can remember, I believed in being in the moment. This enabled me to mentally record events and file them in my Spirit. I use the term spirit since it operates outside the realm of space and time. Although I was born in New York City, at the age of two, we moved to my mother's hometown In Western Pennsylvania. Franklin was the total opposite of where I was first introduced to the world. It was a little rural town like the kind you would see on a post card or a Norman Rockwell painting.

Unfortunately, the demographics did not favor the African American, known back then as 'Colored'. During the 1950's and 60's colored folk in that town were considered second class and treated accordingly. Being a small fraction of the population, many colored folks were related which resulted In slim dating prospects. At the same time interracial dating was taboo.

It was under these social conditions that I predicted that a colored girl would come to Franklin, that I would marry her, and she would give me a son on my birthday, May 21. I made this prediction, or prophecy when I was about ten years old. I did not believe it would ever come true.

CHAPTER TWO

Franklin Life

As I look back over it, there were many things I hated about my life growing up in Franklin. As if being Colored was not bad enough, we were beneath the social-economic standards in every way possible: we did not have a father, we were on welfare, we never had a car, we lived in a shack, and the list of negatives continued. Out of all the negatives, the lack of our mother's concern for the development of her children stood out. By the time she had returned to Franklin she already had five children by four different men. She had given up her first daughter for adoption, gave her second daughter her father's name, then met and married my father and had my older brother and me. She then had another baby with a man from The Bronx, NY. and gave him my father's name.

When she returned to Franklin, she had two more daughters and gave them their father's name. Then she met another man and had two daughters and a son and gave them all my father's name. During the time she was living with this man, she got pregnant by another man, had a daughter, and once again, gave her my father's name.

After 20 years of this messy life, my older brother died in Viet Nam, she finally divorced our father, and married the man who was father of hree of her children. At the age of 43, she gave birth to her 12th child who became the only one of his father's four children bearing his name. All the events occurred while living in the same shack.

Living in a small town where everyone knows your business was also a continuous issue I had to deal with. The cops were at our house every other weekend over some form of domestic violence. Our house was the party house where my mother's relatives and friends gathered to fellowship in their own tribal way. One of the most embarrassing episodes was when my older sister got pregnant in the 12th Grade. She became the first pregnant student in our school.

CHAPTER THREE

Hold Your Head Up

Although it was a struggle to maintain some sense of dignity under humiliating circumstances, I was blessed with internal survivor skills. Somehow, I knew that family conditions did not define me.

When I was four years old, I made a mark on a piece of paper with a pencil. I soon discovered I could make that mark look like something in my mind. It was at that point I found my way to express my self through awareness. Drawing became a form of escape from the harsh reality of my young life. I was able to imagine how I would live in the future. Through my art, I became my best friend.

During my childhood and adolescence, I developed a degree of confidence which made me stand out In a crowd. It was important for me to recognize my worth as a human being and work on things which enhanced self-esteem. In High school my extracurricular activities included: French Club, Radio Club, Student Council, Varsity Club, Cross Country, Track, and captain of the Wrestling Team. Despite my family's reputation, I still held my head up. I was the only male in the family to graduate from high school and college.

We cannot choose our family nor how we start out in life. Everyone at some point must become responsible for their life. Blaming others for your choices is just a waste of time. All my half siblings accused me of thinking I was better than them. I am not better than anyone else. However, I believe in establishing standards that enhance your life and represent your identity.

CHAPTER FOUR

Transition

Under the conditions, I considered the first 18 years of my life as basically normal. One of the few highlights was when George W. Daniels, Sr., Georgie, and my father, came with intent to take us. His attempt failed since our loving mother claimed she was going to need us. What we needed meant nothing to her. My older brother really needed his father and without him, died at the early age of Twenty. If our parents had been concerned about our welfare, provisions would have been made for our father to be a part of our lives. Oh well.

Another highlight was meeting Gretchen halfway through my Senior year. This meeting was significant in many ways. I became aware of my Being in a manner which opened the door to a realm of infinite possibilities. From a social perspective, I became known for breaking the color barrier by openly dating a white girl. More importantly, being accepted by her mother, enabled further assimilation into the White core culture. Gretchen's birthday was August 19th. For some reason, this date was awfully familiar. Later, its significance would be revealed.

During my final year of high school, Ms. Feldman, my English Teacher requested I stay after class. This woman was wise and experienced in life. She had graduated from Vasser University and had served as an Army Officer during World War Two. I will never forget what she told me with her deep blue eyes giving a stern look. She stated, "Stephen, when you graduate, leave this town and don't look back." Apparently, she was aware of my dysfunctional family and was instructing me to save myself. I only wish I had understood. It took years and a lot of pain to realize I did not have a family.

CHAPTER FIVE

Identity Crisis

After years of being socialized in a white world, getting out and interacting with those who looked like me would prove challenging. Initially, I was ridiculed for sounding like a white boy. Although the black girls found me attractive, I was afraid of them. This was based on my misguided ideas of what constituted beauty. It was sad that I had grown up thinking a female had to be white to be beautiful.

Out of all the revelations experienced in my life, realizing the diverse beauty of black women stands out. After years of being brainwashed by the white standard of beauty, I was finally free of many stereotypical patterns. This resulted in a new self-concept. I no longer wanted what I was told I should have. I did not need a song, chant, or slogan to remind me that I was a Human Being.

Based on my developed communication skills, I was able to relate across racial lines. Many of my black friends did not understand that I also had white friends. People thought I had a middle class background based on the way I talked and carried myself. Although I was born in poverty, poverty was not born into me.

Yes, it was somewhat of a struggle to deal with those who perceived me as not being black enough. It was important for me to accept myself for who I was. There was no need to meet others' expectations.

Locations which helped develop my identity included: Boston, MA., Millersville State University, PA., Edinboro State University, PA., and Los Angeles, CA. Overall, I learned that my real profession was finding my way to myself.

CHAPTER SIX

The Road to Renee

Remember that nothing comes out of a vacuum. Everything that happens is caused by previous actions. Such is the case with meeting Renee, the girl in my prophecy. Sylvia Renee Graves was born February 17, 1957. She was the first child of Richard and Adele Graves. If I recall correctly, her place of birth was either Hackensack or Englewood, New Jersey. During her early years, she was in the middle of a turbulent marriage in which she became the pawn. Richard's father allegedly used a shotgun and threatened Adele to stay off his property. They had little Renee and accused Adele of not being a good mother. Richard was in the Army during this time.

They later settled in Paterson, New Jersy and had three more children, one of whom was a result of an extra marital affair. Renee and her mother never got along. It was if Adele resented her for some reason. Renee was always a cute little girl with deep dimples. She would not grow any taller than 4 ft. 11 inches and had a very sweet demeaner. In ways, she was like a living baby doll. She also spoke in a very pleasant and soft voice. Sugar would not melt in her mouth.

Have you ever heard the phrase, "Looks can be deceiving"? Well, the description of Renee is somewhat misleading. First, she became promiscuous at an early age and was attracted to men twice her age.

Secondly, she was a problem for her parents since she was always in the streets. Thirdly, she allegedly had a few abortions before she had reached seventeen. Although she claimed being a good student with plans on attending Tuskegee University and becoming a veterinarian, that was nothing more than a pipe dream.

When Richard's brother, James married my third cousin, Ermagene, all hell was about to break loose. The first time I saw Renee was at the wedding reception. She stood out with her cute appearance and the way she danced. Anyone could tell she was a city girl. Her parents liked the small-town atmosphere of Franklin and thought it would be a safe place to keep their wild daughter out of trouble.

CHAPTER SEVEN

Introduction to Hell

In 1973, after two years of college and a year living in Los Angeles, I returned to Franklin. At the age of twenty-two, I was still young and uncertain about my future. One thing was certain, I did not want to end up in Franklin. I had a few jobs which offered a future, but they were not for me. During the Summer of 1974, I obtained employment at Polk Institute. This was a state hospital that provided care for severely special needs individuals. The job I had was under a summer program designated for college students.

Renee's Uncle James coordinated with her parents to get her to visit Franklin for the summer. As luck would have it, she also got a summer job at Polk. As soon as she got to Franklin, she hooked up with Ermagene's little brother, Richard 'Rocky' Collins. Within a week they committed to a five year engagement. This would legitimize their intimate relationship. Renee was seventeen and Rocky was twenty-one. Getting with Rocky should have raised a huge red flag! Not only did it show how promiscuous she was, but also her low standards. Rocky had a serious hygiene problem and a reputation for being allergic to soap.

As the script goes, Renee and I ended up working together and got know each other. We started playing around when I noticed another red flag. She could get mad very easily and could not control her emotions.

Once she attacked me with the lid of a metal garbage can and tried to knock me out! Her temper could go from zero to sixty in a flash often resulting in a violent act. This problem would persist throughout the time I knew her. Getting back to her attraction to older men.

Although Rocky was four years older and I was six years older than Renee, we were just boys. For some reason she liked men her father's age. During her summer in Franklin, she found a man who could give her what she wanted. His name was Theodore 'Ponch' Lawrence and was twenty years her senior. Although she tried to keep it a secret, people in that small town knew where her walks down 14th street led to.

As the summer passed, working together brought us closer. We would even lay in the grass and study images of the white fluffy clouds floating above us. Yes, it was a time of innocence surrounded by hot passionate lust. One day, nearing the edge of our time together, she changed the narrative. Renee appeared at work wearing a revealing red hot halter top. This created our first and only interaction in the apple orchard. It was another red flag which I chose to ignore. How could she get with me when she was engaged and intimate with my cousin?

Getting with me that day was premeditated with willful intent. If she could betray Rocky, how long would it take to betray me? Unfortunately, I was stupidly falling in love with her, and I ignored all the flags. I compared myself to a heroin addict, taking pleasure in a temporary fix without thinking about the long-term consequences.

CHAPTER EIGHT

Out of the Frying Pan....

The concept of falling in love needs to be fully examined. It's no different than falling in some manure. This is a state of mine where logic is replaced by hormones and desires. There may be hundreds of red flags warning you to stay away, but your stupid emotions overrule. We become our worse enemy and have no one else to blame. As I write this story, I cannot over emphasize my accountability.

After the apple orchard encounter, since she was still engaged to Rocky, all efforts were made to keep us apart. At least during the rest of her Franklin visit. I did have the opportunity to give her my denim jacket. This jacket had my astrological sign (Taurus/Gemini) painted on the back. Ermagene and her family were very upset about Renee having the jacket. They believed it was possessed and instructed her to immediately return it to me. If the jacket had been possessed, it was too late to return it. Its purpose was fulfilled.

At the end of summer, Renee went back to her home in Paterson. We acknowledged how we felt about each other and sustained our relationship via telephone and letters. It was around the end of September when I asked if I could visit her in Paterson. I'll never forget her response, she said, "Yes, Yes, Yes!". I was excited and thrilled at the idea of seeing her and meeting her family.

Sometimes God will give you what you want, but not the way you want it. In October, I borrowed my mother's car and made the five-hour trip to Paterson. There was a hard rain most of the trip, however, it could not erase the sunshine in my mind. Seeing Renee again was all that mattered. When I arrived in Paterson, I started looking for 238 19th Avenue. After some time, I thought I had found it. As I recall it was in an upper middle-class neighborhood. I was not only impressed but a little intimidated. When I reached the door, the resident informed me I was on the wrong side of town. Finding the right address on the East side opened my eyes to my new reality.

CHAPTER NINE

She said, "Yes, Yes, Yes"

The rest of this story is full of questions that remain unanswered. My life changed from the moment I arrived and was introduced into Renee's world. I met her father, Richard, a Deacon in his church, her mother, Adele, who also held a position in the church, her twelve-year-old sister, Regina, and her nine-year-old twin siblings, Ricky and Ramona. They lived on the second floor of a large house owned by Richard. He rented the first and third floors.

Based on the parents both serving God and Richard being wise enough to invest in a house which provided extra income, one would think the foundation of the family structure would be solid. If there were any problems facing the family, the parents with God's guidance, would seek sound resolution.

The father, man of God, head of household, provider, protector, and overall, a good Steward, was not a part of this script. Renee waited until after I made the trip to inform me that she was pregnant. No sooner than she had returned to Paterson, she had gotten pregnant! All the time we had been talking about our developing relationship, she had been laying with a man old enough to be her father. If she had been honest, she would have told me before I made the trip to see her.

Withholding such significant information was part of her mode of operation. She figured that telling me in person would be to her favor, since she could use her 'sweetness' to make It appear acceptable. In her mind, she could do no wrong. She never felt remorse or the need to apologize. If you caught her in the wrong, she would find a way to penalize you.

Renee withholding the fact that she was pregnant was problematic. However, the fact that her parents were well aware of her predicament was exceptional. Normally, the parents would not allow another man to come visit their young pregnant daughter in their home unless he was the father. They knew I was not the father. The father's name was Earl who was thirty-seven years old. What were these people of God thinking? What was the purpose of involving me in their mess?

They assumed, based on my small-town naivety and being madly in love with their daughter, I would overlook the pregnancy. They had grown tired of Renee's promiscuous ways. God only knows how many times they had to take her to abortion clinics. I was the best candidate to take the problem out of their hands. I was not aware of their real agenda. I had just wanted to visit Renee. I had no other intentions.

As a young man, I was not thinking about settling down. I did not know the purpose of my visit was to take Renee with me when I left. As I look back, everything had been set up for that very thing to occur. Noteworthy events that took place during my visit:

- Renee informed me of her pregnancy after I arrived
- Renee sneaking into my bed even though pregnant with another man's child
- Parents condoning my visit while daughter is pregnant
- Adele treating Renee like a stepchild
- Richard's fatal attempt to convince Earl to marry Renee*

- Renee leaving with Earl and stays out for about six hours**
- Adele's party, was this a farewell party for Renee?***

*Saturday afternoon during my visit. Earl and Richard sat in the dining room discussing the pregnancy. Richard wanted Earl to marry his young daughter and even offered financial assistance. Earl's position was that he could not marry Renee since he was already living with a woman and they had three children. There was no further negotiating.

Earl was about the same age as Richard. Richard, being the father and a man of God should have taken a stronger stance. Renee was seventeen, a minor. The parents would have been within their rights to file charges based on statutory rape. Obviously, they did not care that much about their daughter.

**Even though I was supposed to be Renee's guest, she left with the man who got her pregnant and stayed gone for hours. What were they doing, saying their last goodbyes? She demonstrated a total disregard for me and did not care what I thought. The fact that I was there, meant absolutely nothing to her.

***I am not sure why Adele hosted a party. I remember her preparing fried chicken, potato salad, etc., and there was plenty to drink. Some of the people in attendance were Olivia, Richard's sister, Marilyn and Charles, Adele's sister and brother, and I also met Regina's father. Richard was not there since he was against having alcohol in his home. Adele did not care what Richard like or did not like. The next she threw a beer bottle at him after he grumbled about alcohol. I believe the purpose of this party was to bid farewell to Renee.

During the time Renee had left with her man, Earl; Richard had plenty opportunity to say to me, "Young man, I am sorry I allowed you to visit my home under these circumstances. My family issues should not be your concern. Can't you see my daughter does not care about you? Not only did she get pregnant by another man, she left you to spend time with him while you are here. You may think you are in love with her, but you are just a small-town fool. As a man of God, I am ordering you out of my home immediately. This is for your own good. Leave Paterson and do not look back!" "Even though I love my daughter, she's no good for you. If you try to make a life with her, she will do her best to destroy you. It's in her nature. Don't walk but run as fast and far away as you can."

If Richard Graves had truly been a man of God, he could have saved me from his daughter. He knew she would abuse my love and cause immeasurable misery. When I first asked Renee if I could visit her, she responded, "Yes, Yes, Yes". Her first yes meant, "I'm pregnant with another man's baby." Her second yes meant, "You'll be my Knight in shiny armor". Her third yes meant, "I'm going to abuse you for the rest of your life."

CHAPTER TEN

Scandalous

During my short visit, it became apparent that poor sweet little Renee was a victim of family abuse. She wanted to escape Paterson, and I, unknowingly, had been chosen to facilitate her mission. As I reflect, it appeared her parents helped coordinate and support using me to relieve them of their problem child.

I was leaving Paterson on Sunday, the day after Adele's party. We had left the party and went to Renee's Uncle Charles apartment. Charles was about my age and loved to drink. We spent the rest of Saturday night at his place and returned to Renee's home Sunday morning. We arrived to an empty home since everyone had gone to church. I cannot recall the content of our conversation which resulted in her packing her clothes, getting some food for the trip, and leaving her home with me.

She was only seventeen, pregnant, and traveling back to Pennsylvania with me. From a legal perspective, I was a twenty-three transporting a seventeen-year-old pregnant minor across state lines. Even though she was going on her own volition, it still could be considered kidnapping.

When Renee's parents returned from church and realized their daughter had left with me, they should have called the State Police and reported their sweet innocent daughter had been kidnapped. They also should have filed charges against the man who had impregnated her, but they did not. In both instances, loving parents would have taken legal action. For some unknown reason, Renee's parents chose not to involve Law Enforcement. What was wrong with these God-fearing people? Could it be Renee had a valid reason for running away?

I lived in an apartment in Oil City, PA., which is 8 miles from Franklin. We arrived early Monday morning and went to bed. Here I am lying in my bed with a runaway minor who is pregnant with another man's baby. What was I thinking? How in the world did things happen so fast? That morning, we were wakened by knock on the door. It was Renee's Uncle James. Her parents had called him and asked that he confirm that she was with me. They talked for a little while.

Renee explained herself in a way James seem to understand. He left and reported back to her parents. This situation warranted family intervention.

CHAPTER ELEVEN

Guess Who's Coming to Dinner?

During this turbulent time, I had been employed at Polk State Hospital as a Care Provider. The pay was decent, but the job sucked. Adding Renee and her issues to the mix was not a very smart move. My stress level continued to increase. I kept thinking about what I was going to do with another man's baby. Hell, I did not even want a baby of my own. Still, all I had to do was look at sweet little Lolita, I mean Renee, my heart would melt, and I knew everything was going to be alright. The pregnancy was looking good on her.

The first week we were in PA., everything was a blur. I was not sure if I was coming or going. My family all loved Renee. She wooed them with her sweet baby doll charm. Danny, my mother's common law husband just adored her. My mother was the only one who knew about the pregnancy. It did not seem to bother her. Renee had told her how she was sick and had taken too much medication. She felt it was best to have an abortion since there was a possibility the baby would come out deformed. This was her prognosis without any medical input.

Sunday, we were all having dinner at the family home in Franklin.

Normally, if one plans to visit they call first to make sure it is a good time. While we were eating and having fellowship, Renee's parents and uncles, Rosevelt and James came to the house. They were welcomed and seated in the living room. Rosevelt allegedly had carried a gun in case there was in trouble.

They say if you do not take time do things right the first time, you will have to take time to do it over again. This whole situation could have been prevented if Richard had not allowed me to visit his pregnant daughter. This point cannot be overemphasized. As a father, Richard was derelict of his responsibilities which resulted in his making a long trip to Franklin. This only further questioned the relationship between him and Renee.

We all sat in the living room discussing the issues and trying to produce viable solutions.

Those present included, Renee's parents and uncles, my mother and her husband, Renee, and me. Things became tense when Renee's parents started talking about their daughter like she was a whore out on the streets. I must give Danny credit for standing up and emphatically stating, "You are not going to talk about that young lady like that in my home!" It is interesting that her parents would make a long-distance trip only to demean their daughter in front of strangers. It is also interesting that Renee never spoke a word. Could it be her silence supported her parent's description of her?

In conclusion, her parents wanted her to come back home until she reached the legal age of eighteen. Then she would be allowed to make her own decisions. It is funny how the elephant in the room, her pregnancy was not mentioned. She reluctantly agreed to return to Paterson but, did not return with her parents. She stayed with me for another week and then took the bus back to Paterson where she would have the abortion and return to me after her 18th birthday. Since her birthday was February 17th; she would still have half of her senior year in high school to complete.

What was so important about being with me that she would want to leave her home and family and not finish her senior year of high school? Even as I write this, I cannot help but wonder what were the basis of her decisions.

The actual time we had spent together prior to her leaving her home and family was minimal. We had only communicated face to face during the short summer we had worked together. There was never sufficient time for developing a relationship. All the events transpired without any logical basis. It was if there were outside forces creating this unusual relationship. Was it our fate or destiny?

CHAPTER TWELVE
Possible Reasons

I have always wanted to understand the root causes of events which happen in my life. Having a photographic memory has helped immensely in putting pieces together. This has resulted in comprehending causality from a larger perspective. It should be noted that the characters in this book are not guilty of any willful acts. Each performed their role in accordance with a larger scheme. This does not necessarily exonerate them since all actions were made by choice.

This book is written based on the theory that we are all a part of an ongoing Spiritual Warfare. In this scenario, allies and adversaries, as well as good and evil become difficult to identify. Hopefully, the players in this story will be able to recognize themselves and their roles, and understand the underlying spiritual dynamics. When considering the possible reasons for the unusual relationship between Renee and me, I would like to address the following:

(1) the early prophecy; (2) the conception/birth concept: (3) the Jimi Hendrix influence; and (4) the blue denim jacket.

— Early Prophecy: as a young boy, I had prophesized about a girl coming to my hometown, that I would marry her, and she would bear my son on my birthday.

— Conception/Birth Concept: the average number of days between conception and birth is 280 days (nine months). There is a connection between Renee and me based on our birthdays.

Mine is May 21st and her's is February 17th. There are 271 days between our birthdays. This shows a strong possibility that Renee was conceived on, or about the day I was born. Although we Don't normally place any emphasis on time of conception, it remains a crucial factor since birth can not occur without it.

— The Jimi Hendrix Influence: I have briefly discussed my first girlfriend, Gretchen. Her birthday Is August 19th. For some reason this date always stood out. This is because I was conceived on, or about the day of her birth. There are 274 days between our birthdays. This date would further be confirmed by my son being conceived on August 19th and being born on my birthday. Gretchen's impact on my life was significant in many ways, especially her love of music. Out of all the artist I was exposed to, Jimi Hendrix was exceptional. His music and lyrics reflected my life. At the time, I felt he had possessed my soul. Even though our time spent together was short, it was heavily influenced by the spirit of Jimi Hendrix. Foolishly as I recall, Renee would often tell me how she thought I was Jimi Hendrix!

— The Blue Denim Jacket: I had painted my astrological sign, (Taurus/Gemini) on the back of this jacket and gave it to Renee. This would confirm the prophecy that she would bear my son on my birthday.

Despite all the red flags, unfortunately this story was allowed to continue. It is my opinion that our relationship was damned from the beginning. If I had the chance to do it over again, I would not. The old folks use to say, "If it does not start right, it will not end right."

CHAPTER THIRTEEN

March 2, 1975, 'The Day of Infamy'

Disregarding all the red flags, prophecy still had to be fulfilled. Stephen Mott Daniels and Sylvia Renee Graves were meant to be together. If this was true, only God knew why, and He was not talking.

On February 17, 1975, Renee reached her eighteenth birthday and could not wait to leave Paterson and return to me. She had brought her school documents, her luggage, and most importantly, she had aborted Earl's baby. I was somewhat concerned about how she handled her abortion. She spoke about it like it was a simple procedure and no big deal at all. I could not help but wonder if she had previous abortions. I buried those thoughts and just enjoyed being with her again.

Our life living in sin was short lived. My mother claimed to be a Christian serving God and thought it was wrong for us to live together without being married. Instead of advocating marriage, I wished she had cared enough to convince me to get as far away from Renee as I could. She was well aware of Renee's lack of a moral compass. Renee had no conscience nor need to show remorse. She would demonstrate strong psychopathic tendencies throughout the time I knew her.

On March 2, 1975, two weeks after her eighteenth birthday, we were married. This day would forever be my day of infamy. I wished I had a relationship with someone wise who I respected and would listen to. There was no one who cared enough to intervene. I was on my way to be slaughtered and did not even know it.

CHAPTER FOURTEEN

James' Monkey

When Renee had returned, she had her luggage, a small black and white television, and a cute little monkey doll. She was extremely attached to this monkey since it had been given to her by the love of her life, James Bethea. This was nothing but another red flag. She had entered our marriage while still in love with James Bethea. It was obvious that her love for him never prevented her involvement with other men and even getting pregnant by them.

Renee had once told me how it did not matter who she married because her life would end up the same. I was a little offended by that statement. What did she really mean? It appeared her views were based on her parents' loveless marriage. As I reflect over her life, it was full of bad choices, which solidified her negative outlook.

On the other hand, I was idealistic and saw Renee as my Queen. I had a vision of a beautiful marriage, home, and family. I had wanted to grow old with my wife. As an artist, I believed I could turn visions into reality. Anything was possible as long as we stood in one accord. together will could work towards constantly improving our quality of life.

Renee had many fine attributes. She was a seamstress, loved animals, had good social skills, was good in the kitchen and had a strong work ethic. She bought her first car, a little white Ford Falcon, when she was sixteen. In most of her relationships, she had the role of Bread winner. She accepted having mates who did not do their part. When we were first married, I had been terminated from my job (02/14/1975) for calling my supervisor a red neck bigot. I filed a discrimination complaint and took a lower paying job.

During this time, Renee was competing her senior year at Oil City High School. I was her husband and guardian. After graduating that summer, she was employed as a nurse's aide at Oil City Hospital. Once my unemployment benefits expired. She became our sole source of income.

Living in rural areas in Western PA., it was difficult for me to obtain meaningful employment. At the same time I was uncomfortable leaning on my young wife's income. I knew I had to do something to change the conditions as well as my life. This resulted in my decision to enlist in the United States Air Force. This decision would bring many trials and tribulations and prove to be the most rewarding move I would make in my life.

I was scheduled to attend Basic Training In November 1975. We moved back to Franklin a couple of months prior to my departure and stayed at my mother's house. Renee got a nurse's aide job at Franklin Hospital and would wait until I completed Basic Training. On November 3, 1975, I flew from Pittsburgh to San Antonio, Texas and arrived at Lackland AFB early the next morning.

CHAPTER FIFTEEN

A Look at the US Air Force

Prior to enlisting into the Air Force, I did my due diligence and considered the other military services: The Army, Navy, and the Marines. They were all great organizations, but I felt I was a better fit in the Air Force.

The Air force was established September 18, 1948, under the National Security Act. This modern military organization which originated from the Army Air Corp, placed importance on developing its members to effectively accomplish a highly technologized mission. Emphasis on individual development benefitted the mission as well as enhancing professional growth. The individual was given opportunities to excel in job performance while achieving their personal goals.

One of the most important features of this new military organization was its structure with built in flexibility for change which encouraged member input. Being under the Federal government required compliance with all laws, regulations, and policies, most importantly, the US Constitution. Still, the Air Force was not free of discriminatory practices. In the early seventies the Federal Government started establishing Affirmative Action Programs. They were intended to right the wrongs of past discrimination.

The Air Force had a quota system which limited enlisted minorities. Those who were selected to enlist were often assigned to lower support positions like, cooks, fuels, supply, transportation, and security police. This resulted in an over representation of minorities in lower performance fields.

When I enlisted in 1975, anyone with at least two years of college was given two stripes and promoted to A1C (E3). My Caucasian recruiters withheld this information resulting in me starting with no stripes and being an Airman Basic (E1). I had become a victim of their discrimination from the beginning. After completing Basic Training, I was assigned to Fuels, another institutional discrimination practice. Even though I had joined the Air Force to escape discrimination. I only found it on a larger scale.

Working in the Fuels field made me a double minority. The job consisted of handling motor gas, diesel, and jet fuel. The fumes from these fuels permeated our uniforms resulting in other members treating us like second class citizens. Not only did we refuel and defuel all jets and planes, we also provided fuel to all government vehicles assigned to the base. I was so disgusted with my job that I was seriously thinking about getting out of the Air Force.

It was at that time Renee said something which made me rethink everything. "What are you going to do?" she asked. "Go back to Franklin and do what?" Her statement hit me like a ton of bricks.

I could have been stupid, ignored her, and found a way to get out of my enlistment. However, I was fortunate to be able to listen and accept my reality. Unfortunately, Renee did not realize she was part of the team and had her own responsibilities to fulfill.

After Renee brought me to my senses, I began to see things differently. If I did not like the job I had; I would take the opportunity to get a better job. With my new attitude I moved from directly handling fuel to becoming a Fuels accountant. After that, I became the lowest ranking member to attend and graduate from Fuels Laboratory School.

In 1979 while stationed in Japan, I was notified that I was eligible to cross train under the Air Force Affirmative Action Program. The Air Force recognized the Fuels field was overrepresented with minorities and had to come up with a viable solution. I was provided with a short list of fields which included Social Actions. At this time, I became a candidate for the Social Actions Program.

The Air Force Social Actions Program was established to ensure all members were given an equal opportunity to succeed. There had been many publicized riots on military installations including the Kitty hawk, Fort Dix, and McQuire AFB. The issue of racial unrest within the Department of Defense required immediate response and resolution. Consequently, the Social Actions Program was established and empowered to combat racism, discrimination, Sexual harassment, and enhance the human relations climate throughout the Air Force Organization.

After completing the 16-week course at the Defense Equal Opportunity and Management Institute, (Patrick AFB, FL.), I started my Social Actions career at Davis-Monthan AFB, AZ. I was no longer a part of a squadron but worked directly for the Base Commander. My job came with high visibility and a perceived position of power. As a representative of Air Force Equal Opportunity and Treatment (EOT) policies, it was imperative to maintain a high standard of professional appearance and excellent speaking skills.

My responsibilities included teaching Human Relations and Sexual Harassment Awareness, processing discrimination complaints, conducting organizational assessments, maintaining Affirmative Actions Statistics and monitoring the installation human relations climate.

My experience in Social Actions enhanced my self-worth and self-esteem and increased my confidence. After six years, I applied for and became a Professional Military Education (PME) Instructor. In this position, I prepared young Airmen for supervisory roles. As Commandant, (Program Manager) of Airman Leadership School (ALS) I was awarded the Air Force Achievement Medal by General McDonald, Commander, Air Force Logistics Command (AFLC). This award was based on creating a uniquely designed PME center which included painted murals of Air Force scenes. My twenty-year Air Force career was instrumental in my overall development. The structured Thought process, like management by objectives, is something I apply in everyday life. Questioning, analyzing, researching, and thinking creatively have all originated from the Air Force culture. From a social perspective, I have been able to assimilate to our nation's core culture. I no longer accept exceptional treatment based on subjective factors. I have learned how to fight to win. My thought process has been crystalized. I now use my pen as my lethal weapon.

CHAPTER SIXTEEN

One Step Closer

As I wrote this true story, I realized most of it evolved around the twenty years I spent in the Air Force (1975-1995). Again, it is important to note that the people mentioned in this book are not guilty of anything. They were only actors playing out their roles and making their exit.

As I had previously stated, I had completed Basic Training, been assigned to Fuels, Sheppard AFB, Wichita Falls, TX., and traveled to Franklin prior to reporting for duty. It was good reuniting with Renee. The Band, Rufus featuring Chaka Khan had just come out with their new hit, 'Sweet Thing' and it became our theme song. We spent less than a week together since I had many things to accomplish in Wichita Falls. Along with reporting for duty, I had to purchase a vehicle and find a place for us to live. Renee would be arriving within two weeks.

The Air Force Sponsor Program was set up to help new assignees make a smooth transition. My sponsor was Sgt. Robert Gonzalez. He assisted in looking for a car and an apartment.

I got a 1972 Plymouth Duster financed through the Sheppard AFB Federal Credit Union and rented a one bedroom furnished apartment on the eastside which was also known as 'Colored Town'.

The apartment complex was called, King's Square Apartments, 1520 Trout Street, Wichita Falls, Texas. This would be the location where our marriage would develop and fall apart in less than a year.

Renee arrived in early January 1976 and was pleased how I had prepared everything for her. She had a husband who was committed to her and knew how to take care of business. Along with her luggage and little television, she also brought the little monkey James Bethea had given her.

The first couple of months were good for her. I got up and went to work and she had time to catch up on her soaps. In time, we realized that if we wanted more she would also have to work. She obtained employment as a Nurse's aide at Wichita Falls General Hospital.

Our apartment was under Federal Subsidized Housing which meant the rent was cheap and included utilities. It was not long before we decided to rent a two-bedroom unfurnished apartment. We laid away all the furnishings including a living room set, dinette, and nice bedroom set. Through our diligence, we were able to reach our goal and within two months, be in our new furnished home. We had the potential to reach many goals as a team.

Before I go any further, I must say that I hate roaches. I refuse to live with them and will take all measures to eliminate them from my environment. The idea of them crawling all over me when I'm sleeping is totally unacceptable. Prior to moving into our new apartment, we painted and sprayed to insure their elimination. I could not understand how some people are comfortable living with these filthy pests. During the time I lived in apartment 2-B, there were no roaches.

Cleanliness was the best way to combat them.

CHAPTER SEVENTEEN

"Operator, who's been calling?"

Whenever people want to be exonerated from their actions, they always say something about that being in the past. This book is a good example of how the things we do yesterday catch up with us today. In the spiritual realm there is no space and time. Our lives are a tapestry of the past, present, and future.

Our life in Wichita Falls was refreshing and full of promise. We both went to work every day, attended church at Mt. Pleasant Missionary Baptist Church, did our shopping at Piggly Wiggly and Sykes Center Mall; and I attended Midwestern State University. We would go out dancing at the Airmen's Club. Most of our friends were associated with our jobs. People were always impressed with our home. This was a time of peace and contentment.

Whenever things are going too good in your life, you better watch out. Something is always lurking around the corner ready to rain on your parade. One evening while we were home, the telephone kept ringing. Renee would answer it and tell the person they got the wrong number. After the third or fourth time, I told her to give me the phone.

It was the operator informing me that someone had been calling our number using a stolen phone card. They had traced the caller's location to an Army post. I remembered that James Bethea had enlisted in the Army.

I asked Renee about the situation, and she admitted she and James had been talking. She went on to explain that she had wanted to tell me but was afraid how I would react. How long would this have continued if the Operator had not called? I told her things would have been better if she had told me the first time he called. Finding out through the phone operator created a trust issue. Renee blamed her mother for giving James our phone number and accused her of trying to break up our marriage. If this was the case, Renee was helping her mother.

Renee is the kind of person who will penalize you if she is caught doing something wrong. She stopped speaking to me because I found out about her and James. She would act like I did not exist and give me the silent treatment. This was a form of mental abuse. Imagine living in a home with someone who does not acknowledge your existence. Renee never showed any remorse and would make others suffer for her wrongful actions. This character flaw would show up throughout our relationship.

Eventually, things would return to normal as if nothing had happened. Overall, our relationship appeared to be good. In August 1976, we spent a weekend at Lake Texarkana. James and Carole Dix, our close friends went with us. They had recently had their second child, another boy. I felt we were ready to start a family. I will never forget that day, August 19, 1976, while in our cottage I flushed Renee's birth control pills down the toilet. That very day our first child was conceived. I was compelled to take these actions on that given day.

Getting Renee pregnant should have been a joint decision. I took full control of making a decision that would impact both of our lives. Even though she was aware of what was taking place, neither of us were prepared for the consequences.

CHAPTER EIGHTEEN

First Born

Like clockwork, within two weeks Renee started having morning sickness. Keep in mind this was Not her first rodeo so she knew what to expect. I remember taking a photo of her in which she wrote captions, 'I'm going to get him for this.' Although she was smiling in the photo, I believe she meant she was going to destroy me. I must give her credit for taking care of herself throughout the pregnancy. She stopped all alcohol use, no smoking marijuana, she exercised, and was also particular about what she ate. She also demanded we attend Lemans Class every Wednesday evening. At first, I was not crazy about going but there was no way of getting out of it. I had to go and like it too! I did learn about the Importance of the father's role during the pregnancy and giving birth. Renee had decided to breast feed and refused taking drugs for pain while giving birth. She was concerned about them harming our baby. Please note that she was concerned about harming the baby.

Dr. Paul Kinnard, Col, USAF was our obstetrician and was fastidious when it came to Renee's pre-natal care. He was aware of her previous abortion(s) and appropriately counseled us on the care of our newborn. Matters addressed from a psychological perspective included (1) making sure the baby had his own bed; (2) making sure the baby had his own room (if Possible); (3) never let the baby sleep with the parents; (4) it's alright to let the baby cry; and (5) do not spoil the baby. He appeared to imply that some young women who have had abortions try to overcompensate with their first born.

We knew the baby was a boy and that he would be born in May. We agreed he would be named Damian George, after my brother George who died in Vietnam. We had followed Dr. Kinnard's recommendations and made the second bedroom a nursery. We had such a difficult time putting the baby crib together. One night in the month of April, I woke up and then woke Renee. I remember telling her that if the baby was born on my birthday, he would be given my name.

Renee shrugged it off, like fat chance that's going to happen, and went back to sleep.

It was a Friday night, May 20, 1977. Our friends Melvin, Janice and their two children were visiting. They left around 10 and it looked like a storm was heading our way. We went to bed around 11:30, and sure enough, we had a heavy thunderstorm. Around 2 in the morning, Renee woke me stating that her water broke. Before we knew it, I was driving her to Sheppard Regional Hospital. We were going to have our baby on my 26th birthday!

We did not like the title, 'Junior' so we agreed his name would be, Stephen Mott Daniels, II. As I reflect, Renee seemed to hold some resentment that our child had been born on my birthday.

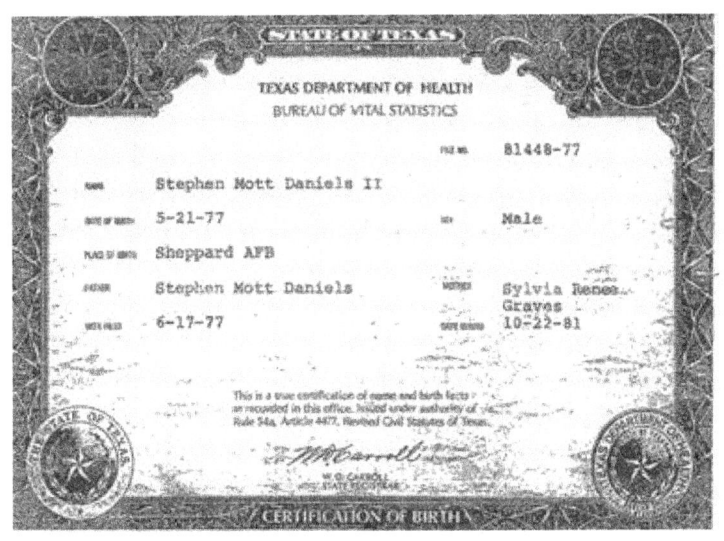

CHAPTER NINETEEN

God Bless this Hell

The novelty of having our first-born child in our home did not last long. Renee had thrown all of Dr. Kinnard's recommendations out the window. Stevie never slept in his own bed because he breast fed. Renee would pick him up if he looked like he was going to cry. Stevie did not cry, he screamed at the top of his lungs. The only bonding that took place was between mother and child. Since I did not have any breasts, the bonding between my son and me was minimal. Stevie learned early how to control his mother through his screaming. Renee was allowing Stevie to control her.

I believe Renee was trying to make up for those she had aborted. I know that may sound cold but, no colder than the act of abortion. I am not saying it's right or wrong, but we must consider the possible psychological factors that can be transferred to the treatment of the first born. This over- compensative treatment can impede the child's development and wreak havoc on the marriage.

Once, what appeared to be a happy home had been replaced by screaming and continuous tension. Being one of the oldest of twelve siblings, I helped raise my younger siblings. I was very familiar with taking care of babies. Stevie's screams were not normal and would literally make a person run out of the house. One Saturday morning in

July, with the normal tension filled atmosphere, Renee decided to take screaming Stevie to the movies. I told her that was not a good idea. (Have You ever gone to the movies and there's a screaming baby in the audience?) Renee replied that I could not tell her what to do.

At that point, I reacted and pushed her. That's when she went crazy. While our baby was sitting on our bed witnessing everything, she picked up a gallon size wine bottle, that had been used as a vase, and with all her strength busted it against my face. She had just missed my left eye. With the baby screaming and blood gushing from my face, she continued her rage. I had to take both her arms and calm her down so she could see what she had done.

When she realized the damage she had caused and how traumatized our baby was, she finally came her senses. My face and shirt covered in blood resulted in her offering to drive me to the Emergency room. Although I was bleeding profusely and could not see out of one eye, I declined her offer and drove myself to the Emergency Room. I told the doctor I had run into a door.

Remember how careful Renee was during pregnancy? She did not want to do anything that would harm the baby. It was obvious her uncontrollable rage traumatized her baby beyond what we could imagine. She is the one who introduced Stevie to blood and violence. Sadly, even to this day, she proudly reminds him of how she almost knocked my eye out. Is being a fool out of control something to be proud of? I should have called the Police and had her arrested for assault with a deadly weapon causing bodily injury and endangerment to a child.

When I returned from the hospital, all stitched up, Renee had prepared a nice Saturday evening meal. this was followed by a night of makeup sex. Although I really cared for her, in my mind I knew this marriage was not going to last. The number of red flags kept increasing representing dangerous roads ahead.

CHAPTER TWENTY

Godsend

Sometimes help can come in unusual ways. News which can appear devastating, can actually be a blessing. Early September, 1977 I received orders to report to Yokota AB, Japan by March 3, 1978. it took a few moments to process this information. Based on my rank, E3, I was not eligible to have my family accompany me. I would have to wait six months before I made E4. At that time The Air Force would pay for my family and household goods to my new location. The assignment length would change from two to four years.

If I had been given two stripes (E3) at the time of my enlistment for having over two years of college, I would have been E4 when I received my orders which would have included my family. This act of discrimination adversely impacted the future of my family.

In order to keep my family together, I was given an opportunity to make E4 through the Below the Zone Board. The morning prior to meeting the Board, Renee and I had an argument leaving me emotionally distraught. Although I performed well in front of the board, I had placed the US insignias upside down on my uniform during the argument I had with Renee. This resulted in not meeting the Board's requirements. If we had been on the same team, Renee would have been helping me to obtain the early promotion. She was a liability who could not enhance my life or my Air Force career.

We had six months before I had to report to my new assignment. There were decisions which had to be made. Renee wanted to stay in Wichita Falls for six months and then accompany me in Japan. She stated she had always wanted to go to Japan. Since my monthly income paid most of the bills including the car, Renee had full access to the account. She would send me Two Hundred dollars a month.

Since I was leaving for Japan in March 1978, Renee wanted to visit her family in Paterson for Christmas. I was against it because we did not have the finances to travel halfway across the country and back. Renee started her silent treatment and continued it until I was forced to get a loan from the credit union.

Driving back east in the winter was a nightmare. Stevie was seven months old and attached to his mother's milk like he was a newborn. As much as Renee had wanted to visit her family, she was no help when it came to driving. The baby would start his screaming if she let him out of her arms.

We stopped and visited my family in PA, and everything was normal. We stayed on the third floor where we use to live. We continued to Paterson. I will never forget this as long as I live. Her parents knew we were coming all the way from Wichita Falls, Texas and showed just how much they cared. They were gracious enough to let us sleep in their bed. However, they did not have the decency to even change the sheets! Renee was visibly embarrassed and humiliated as she put clean sheets on her parents' bed.

I could not help but think about getting the loan, and driving all the way to Paterson without Renee's help only to be treated like a nobody. What kind of people were they? They were always in the Church but what God were they serving? This was nothing more than another red flag. While we were there, Renee and I left Stevie with her parents and went to visit her relatives. It was not loo long before her mother called and demanded we return. Stevie was having a screaming fit and they could not handle it. At least other people knew about the baby's abnormal screaming.

We had fulfilled Renee's desire to travel to see her family. I now had the responsibility to drive back to Wichita Falls while Renee nursed Stevie. It's interesting that she never considered weening him. She continued to breast feed him until her breast became flat as pancakes.

CHAPTER TWENTY-ONE

Them Changes

Since I was married when I enlisted in the Air Force, even as an Airman I had a pretty good life.

I did not live on base and was not subjected to a 24/7 military regulated life. I normally worked five days a week with weekends off. Every month after Commander's Call all the members who resided in the dormitories would have to stay and be briefed on myriad issues pertaining to maintaining a healthy dormitory environment.

I felt privileged to be exempt from that structure and be able to live an ordinary life. Along with my Base Pay, I also received additional allowances for food and housing. The benefits of being married were much better than being a single enlisted member.

The assignment to Japan completely changed my life. I went from a person who had many choices to someone who became controlled by the system. Most importantly, I had been separated from my family. This was a hard pill to swallow. Even if Renee and I were not getting along, I still missed her and Stevie. I went from living in a two-bedroom apartment to being assigned a room in the dormitory with a roommate and community bathroom and showers down the hall. Cleaning toilets, cutting grass, and overall maintenance of the dormitory became part of my responsibility. I was also required to keep my room ready for inspection, which normally occurred on a monthly basis.

My allowance for food was replaced by a meal card. I no longer had a choice on what to eat. Whatever food prepared by the chow hall was the only choice. Another important factor was being on base 24/7. This meant you worked, ate, and slept in facilities like everyone else. On top of all this, I was only getting a small portion of my pay since I still had to support my family. The physical and psychological changes resulted in depression and substance abuse. The assignment to Japan equated to being penalized and I felt like a military prisoner.

Renee had not sacrificed anything. She had become head of household on my dime. She had our furnished apartment, which I was paying for. She had a car to drive which I made the payments. She sent me a monthly allowance of $200. Even though we had agreed they would join me within six months, Renee had no intention of making that happen. Through my assignment, she gained her independence.

Now she could entertain other men in our home, travel back and forth to Ft. Sill to see the soldiers, and party her behind off at the clubs. She saw no need to change as long as she controlled my finances. She never thought about the fact that my unaccompanied assignment would only last two years. What was supposed to happen when I returned home? She was totally apathetic to the conditions I was subjected to and would have continued taking advantage until the train stopped. She never thought the train would arrive early and catch her off guard.

CHAPTER TWENTY-TWO

Renee, what are you going to do?

Remember when I said that help can come in unusual ways? All my life I believe I have had a Guardian Angel, a spiritual entity that guides and protects me. After being in Japan for six months and making E4, I was selected to attend Fuels Accounting School at Chanute AFB, Illinois This five week course would start in September 1978. I had previously completed Fuels Laboratory School at the same base in July 1977. It was amazing that I would be getting an opportunity to go back to the states so soon and the Air Force was paying for it! As part of my itinerary, I included five days of leave so I could see my family in Wichita Falls. I gave Renee notification of when I would be arriving. After completing school, I arrived in Wichita Falls the second week in October. Upon entering the apartment, I felt the home atmosphere had changed. Little did I know what had been going on in my home while I had been gone. The first disturbing thing I noticed was that the roaches had return. It was obvious that Renee's hygiene standards had welcomed the roaches back. This red flag was one of many to come.

On the surface, Renee appeared to be glad to see me and everything was normal. She is a good actress. Stevie was no longer being breast fed but still used his screaming to control his mother. The carpet in the apartment was dirty and our furniture had a funky odor. Renee had let our home go downhill in six months. The week went by fast without any real issues. We went to the circus. Renee had emphasized it would be something we did as a family. Something happened Friday afternoon that got my attention.

The phone rang, and Renee answered it. I did not know who she was talking to but after she finished she said she had something to do and would be right back. I thought it was rather strange. She returned in about an hour and never mentioned what she had to do in such a hurry. The significance of my taking leave at that time was about to be revealed.

It was Sunday morning, the day prior to my flying back to Japan, that I received a phone call that changed my life forever. The caller identified herself as Janice Lacey and she had information I needed to know. She revealed the following:

— — She was the wife of Jimmy Lacey, and he and Renee had been having an affair in my home

— That Renee had taken money to his job at his request

— That Jimmy referred to Renee as 'Sugar' and even Mrs. Lacey

— That she had gone to our apartment to confront Renee and got into a fight

— That Stevie was screaming so loud she got off Renee and cut all the tires on our car

— Renee had her arrested

— Jimmy had called Renee and told her to drop the charges (Friday afternoon call)

— Janice also claimed Renee was having Jimmy's baby

As she told me this disturbing news, it all made sense. I had caught Renee looking in the mirror to see if she was showing. That Friday afternoon phone call was her man, Jimmy directing her to get his wife out of jail. All this news came out in a nick of time. Renee was at work that morning and called me asking if everything was all right. Apparently, Janice had called her and told her that I knew. I told her I knew everything.

When she arrived home, she confessed to the allegations but never mentioned anything about being pregnant. I now understood why she had been asking why I did not have sex with her each night. She was going to claim that I was the father. She told me they would meet in our home since no one had money for a motel. She also told me how she offered to use our bed and how Jimmy said he could not have sex in another man's bed. At least he had some respect which is more than I can say for Renee. She did not have respect for me, our child, our home, or herself.

It is important to note that Stevie was only sixteen months old when he witnessed his mother getting beat up by the wife of her lover. Again, Renee had exposed her child to violence without any consideration for his mental health. Janice Lacey said his screaming and crying was so disturbing that she stopped choking Renee, got up off her, ran down the steps to our car and cut all four tires with the knife she had planned to use on Renee. This incident escalated due to Renee's Insistence that Jimmy Lacey was her man.

She almost got away with it. If Janice Lacey had not called, I would have left the next day not knowing about wretched Renee's latest episodes. I can imagine spending the rest of my assignment in Japan while Renee continued her dirt that I would be financially supporting. During my visit, she had told me the car dealership had told her I was eligible to purchase a new Plymouth Cordoba. She really believed that I would finance a new car for her. That showed the depth of her deceit and selfishness. She had no boundaries. The day I departed; Renee had told me to get out of her apartment.

My name was on the lease, I was paying the rent and we purchased all the furniture together.

The car was in my name, and I had made all the payments. Telling me to vacant her home implied she had been financially independent and did not need my financial support. The idea of taking money to her lover's job was also unacceptable.

During the long flight back to Japan, I had plenty of time to process what had happened. One thing for certain; Renee could no longer be a priority in my life.

CHAPTER TWENTY-THREE

Reconstruction

As I flew across the ocean, I was emotionally devastated. I had lost my home and family and there was nothing I could do about it. Renee's decisions had brought our family to the brink of destruction. her apathy, selfishness, and moral decadence was very evident. It became imperative for me to realize and accept the marriage was over.

For the past six months I had made sacrifices for my family only to face the ultimate betrayal. Renee had claimed that our home and everything we accumulated was her's, I had to relinquish it. This was just one of those disadvantages of being stationed overseas. My car which I had paid for was among the losses. My life in Wichita Falls was fading away.

Many service members in similar situations handle things differently. There are many stories of those who felt their life was over and resorted to destructive measures. They let themselves go never seeing the possibility of a brighter future. I could have been among those who allowed others to dictate their life. I am not advocating the military as the answer to everyone. However, I recognized myriad resources in the Air Force which could aid in my development. It was time to focus on new priorities.

The first thing I did when I arrived at Yokota was visit the Accounting & Finance office. I set up my pay to go directly to my Yokota AB credit union. No longer would Renee have access to any of my finances. Instead of her sending me $200 per month, that is exactly what I would be sending her via Money Orders. She would have serious problems losing control of my pay. Unfortunately, she had lost that privilege due to her poor decisions.

As a result of the financial move, I would be ordered to my Commander's office every month. Renee would contact the Air Force alleging that I was not sending any money. After explaining the situation and showing the money order receipts, Renee's continuous claims fell on deaf ears.

She would write to inform me about her bills. I would write back telling her to get help from her husband, Jimmy Lacey or whoever she had living in HER home.

"Send you all my money. You take it and give it to another man." Women, never, never, never do this! The consequences can haunt you for the rest of your life. Men, if your woman is guilty of this act, run, don't walk from her. It is obvious she means you no good.

Renee had always wanted to have her cake and eat it too. She thought her cuteness gave her license to do whatever she wanted. I thank God, she finally convinced me there was no future with her.

CHAPTER TWENTY-FOUR

Damned from the Beginning

If it does not start right, how can it end right? Though there had been many warning signs, inviting me to visit while she withheld the fact that she was pregnant with another man's baby was the greatest warning sign of all. Her parents should have never allowed this visit but, they did. Every sign contributed to a living evolving monstrous disaster. What more could one expect? Our marriage actually lasted thirty-six months (Mar '75 - Mar 78). I cannot include my two years in Japan since we were separated. They were included for legal purposes. Once Renee realized she no longer had access to my monthly income, she hired an attorney and filed for divorce. Her attorney misled her to believe the divorce could be accomplished.

When I received notification of the divorce, I took it to the Legal office. I was informed that under The Soldiers and Sailors Protection Act I could not be divorced while serving overseas. Renee's attorney knew this but filed anyway. After committing adultery in our home, Renee attempted to exonerate herself by filing for divorce. What did she expect to gain from this frivolous action?

CHAPTER TWENTY-FIVE

Petitioner or Respondent?

On March 2, 1980, I returned to the states and was assigned to Davis=Monthan AFB, Arizona. I would be attending a 16-week school at Patrick AFB, Florida in May. After settling in, I took a five day leave and flew to Wichita Falls where I had left my family. Upon arriving at Kings Square Apartments, to my dismay it resembled a war zone. The unit next to ours had caught on fire resulting in many boarded-up windows. There was no one living in our apartment. I had no knowledge of my family's location.

I went to the Apartment Manager's office which was across the street from our apartment, to Inquire about Renee and my son. She was very upset with Renee stating that she had left owing several months of rent and that her father had moved them back to New Jersey. She shared a wealth of information including Jimmy Lacey staying in our apartment; his wife and Renee's big fight; how other men had frequented the apartment; how Jimmy allegedly helped Renee sell our furniture and my car; how Renee forged my signature on the car title; and how Renee had used some of the proceeds to get an abortion and hire an attorney. Too much to tell the Captain! She also referred me to a good family attorney, Barbara Crampton. I was fortunate to meet with her the next day.

My attorney found that Renee had filed for divorce in Wichita County. This required all matters pertaining to the case be addressed in the same county Court. Renee was no longer in Texas.

She had taken our son and moved out of state without giving me or the court prior notice. Under these circumstances I was able to file as Cross Petitioner. When she filed, she did not list our furniture or my vehicle. My attorney expedited the process which resulted in Renee being treated as the Respondent.

Once locating her in Paterson, New Jersey, she was served and ordered to appear in Wichita County Family Court on April 2 1980. This was few weeks prior to my school start date!

When Renee filed for divorce and then left the state, what did she think was going to happen? Did she think I would try to find her and work on our marriage? Did she think I would come crawling back on my knees? I know she was shocked and surprised when she was served. She never thought she would be ordered to travel back to Texas and appear in court. As a Petitioner, court actions are based on your preference. Renee having to take the long two-day bus trip to Wichita Falls, Texas made her the Respondent. After taking care of business in Wichita Falls, I returned to Arizona where I studied for promotion and waited to appear in court prior to attending school in Florida.

CHAPTER TWENTY-SIX

Goodbye Renee

At last, the glorious day of terminating the marriage from Hell had arrived. We both appeared in Court accompanied by our attorneys. Renee was so mad she would not look my way. Poor thing. The proceedings were quick, and Renee was the only one to give testimony. As she spoke in her soft, sweet voice, she broke down in tears alleging she was a victim of spouse abuse. How could this be since I had been in Japan for the past two years? The Court appeared to ignore her and finished the proceedings. My attorney and I decided not to address the furniture and my car since it would consume time and possible impede attending school. It would be advantageous to take the loss.

Based on my rank of E4, I was ordered to pay $100 a month in child support. Renee had no Intentions of complying with the Court Order. I never saw any community or personal property and I would have to get the decree domesticated in New Jersey to see my son. I would end up obtaining nothing from the marriage. Nothing that is, except my freedom.

As Managing Conservator, Renee was responsible for our son's welfare. Each time I was promoted In the Air Force, she could file for Modification of Child Support during the entire time the Court Order was in effect. This was not a choice but a responsibility that Renee had been remiss of. It is ironic That she would put much effort into frivolous claims attempting to destroy my career, but took no action to increase the amount of child support. Her foolish pride was stronger than her concern for her child's welfare.

When considering that she had forged my signature to sell my car; this was not the first time. While I was in basic training, I had been financially compensated for winning my discrimination case. Once Renee received my check in the mail, which was addressed to me, she should not have opened it.

She should have informed me of its arrival and then asked me if she could open it. We had not been married that long and she should have had the decency to respect my privacy. Instead of doing the right thing, she chose not to inform me, opened my mail, forged my signature on my check, and spent the proceeds. I never knew the amount of money. This was a warning of what was to come from Renee.

Once the proceedings were completed, we were divorced. However, it would not become final until August 1980. I flew to Florida and attended The Defense Equal Opportunity and Management Institute. I was finally free of the worst mistake I made in my life.

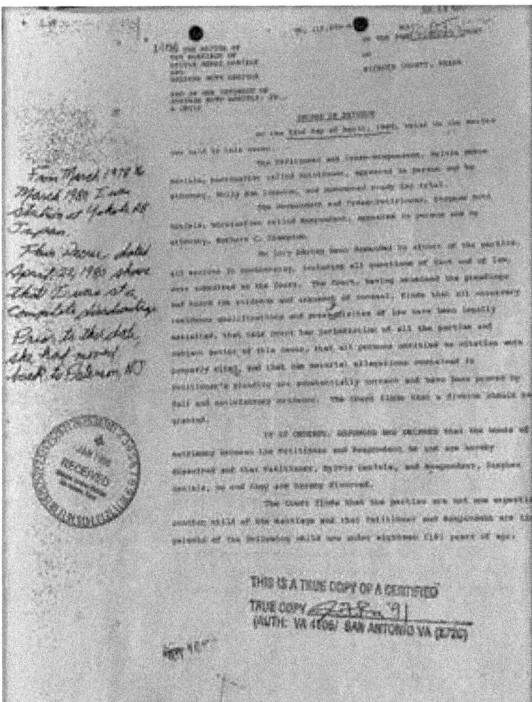

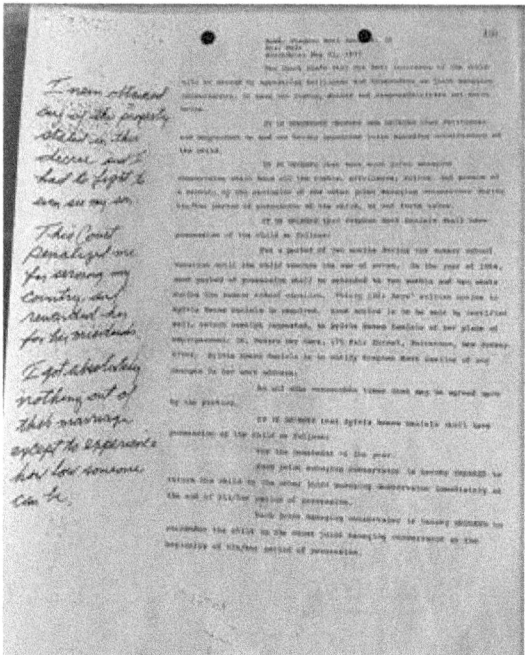
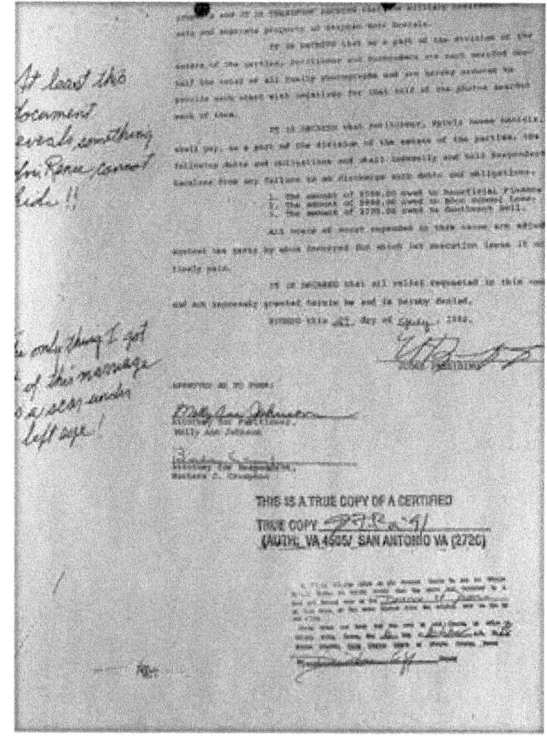

CHAPTER TWENTY-SEVEN

Life after Divorce

Upon gaining freedom from a nightmarish episode in my life, things started falling into place for me. After successfully completing the sixteen-week course in Florida, I returned to Arizona and was promoted to SSgt (E5). I leased a one-bedroom apartment, purchased quality furnishings, and a new car. I did not let my losses from the marriage have any impact on my life. I was at a good position in my Air Force career and I was a bachelor living in Tucson, Arizona.

As far as having a healthy relationship with my son; well, that was a different story. Family Court places emphasis on what is in the best interest of the child. However, many divorced parents don't see it that way. Renee was extremely bitter over the divorce and would use our son against me.

She stood against anything that would enhance the father/son relationship and preferred to have him exposed to a poor quality of life. In many ways our divorce revealed her impoverishment and Ignorance.

Renee had left Paterson while still in high school and was looking for a better life. Instead of committing and fighting to sustain the improvements in her life, she resorted to what she knew and what she was. That may sound harsh but, it is the truth. It is unfortunate that her lifestyle and choices had an adverse effect on our son's development. The following milestones demonstrate and support Renee's impoverishment and ignorance.

— August 1980: Divorce is finalized. Visitation rights are very clear

— May 1981: After giving her notice of visitation, I travel from Tucson to Paterson to see my son on our birthday. She is working at a church daycare and Stevie is with her. To stop me from even touching my son, she attempts to throw a large pot of boiling water on me. Her co- workers witness her behavior, and she was terminated.

— December 1981: Renee contacted me stating that Stevie wants me to visit for Christmas. Keep In mind she tried to toss boiling water on me back in May, now she wants me to come visit her. That does not make sense. I told her I had already made plans and that I would visit Stevie in May for our birthday. She abruptly hung up the phone.

— May 1982: I travel from Tucson to Paterson for us to celebrate our birthday. Renee refused to let me see my son. She was also five months pregnant. If I had visited them in December, She would have claimed that I was the father. That's just how her mind works. Her mother Told me that Kevin Parks was the father. He had lived with Renee in her father's apartment and allegedly abused drugs. He and Renee would have such terrible fights that her father had been forced to put her out. Her mother went on to say that Renee could not count on Kevin, so she was on the hunt. When I failed through, she then found Joe Farrar.June1982: I hired a New Jersey attorney to domesticate our Texas divorce decree. Renee would have to honor my visitation rights

— May 1983: My first visitation with my son. Renee's father had kicked her out due to domestic disturbances. She was living on Park Avenue in the ghetto. Renee married Joe Farrar had given birth to Kevin's son on August 5,1982. She was several months pregnant with Joe's baby. I got to witness just who she was and how far down her life had gone. It was really pitiful. What made it worse was that she had exposed our child to her lifestyle.

— During the time Renee and Kevin lived together, God only knows how much violence Stevie had been exposed to. If the situation warranted her father kicking her out, one can deduce that her violent temper was a contributing factor.

— April 1985: I met up with Renee and her three sons in Paterson. She suggested we all go to DisneyWorld since she had found a discounted package. I agreed and we planned to make

— The trip in July. I purchased the boys' new clothes for the entire stay. Stevie was eight, Andre was three, and Sean was two. I also paid for the DisneyWorld package and our lodging at the Hyatt Islandia. I flew from Alaska to Paterson and then we drove to Florida.

— While Renee was driving, Andre being a three-year-old, was jumping up in down in the backseat. Renee balled up her fist and knocked the little boy to the back of the seat. She still did not know how to control her temper. I think it was on about the third day of our Vacation, we were all in the hotel room. Andre was jumping up and down on the bed and I noticed he was close to the edge. As I reached out to catch him, he fell off the bed. Renee immediately reacted screaming that I had knocked him off the bed! I had no reason to knock him off the bed, but Renee continued to accuse me. She and Stevie were both against me and wanted me out of the room I had paid for. Renee also told me that I was not getting a ride back to Paterson in her car. After all I had done to make the vacation happen, I was treated like Charles Manson out on bail. Not once did I ever hear 'thank you'. I left them at DisneyWorld and flew to Seattle and enjoyed the rest of my vacation before flying back to Alaska where my new woman was waiting for me. When we made this trip, where were the boys' fathers? She was married to Joe and Kevin had never been in the picture.

— May 1987: My new woman and I were married May 1986. We left Alaska and bought a new home in San Antonio Texas in August of the same year. We then had a child in October. Things were going great in my new life until I received a call from Renee. The one who had told me to stay out of their life. She had found out I was married and had a new son. All of the sudden she wanted Stevie to be a part of my life. Knowing what I know now, I should have said 'no'. He did come visit for two weeks.

— September 1991: Renee called stating that Stevie had taken a lot of pills and it was recommended that he live with me. After discussing the matter with my wife, we decided to take him in. During the time he lived with us, he showed no signs of having any mental problems whatsoever. I was pleased to have the opportunity to develop a relationship with him without his mother's influence.

— May 1992: Problems in the marriage. My wife felt trapped and wanted a romantic marriage. The fact that my son was living with us gave her a reason to get out of the marriage. "Either he leaves, or I leave." became her threat which ended the marriage.

During our marital issues, it was decided that Stevie returned to Paterson. We were divorced September 1993 and I was awarded custody of our son, August 1994. Stevie returned to our home and finished out his high school. Just like his mother, he graduated from high school while I was his guardian. What caused him to leave his loving mother and live with me? Like his mom, he also had to attend summer school in order to graduate.

After high school, Stevie decided to enlist in the Air Force. I thought this was a great idea since it would help structure his life. Renee was so proud of our son, and flew to San Antonio for his completion of Basic Training. She stayed in our home during her visit. Unfortunately, Stevie had a difficult time adapting to the Air Force culture. Within two years he was discharged due to mental health issues. Once Renee had been proud of her son. She later blamed me for letting him go in the Air Force knowing he had mental problems.

Once Stevie got out the Air Force, we continued to communicate. He had met a young woman in the Air Force who he got pregnant. He did not want the baby and wanted her to get an abortion. She had the baby without him. Stevie had shared so much about me being the better parent with a sound mind, that she started communicating on a regular basis and would bring the baby for visits.

It is interesting how Stevie omitted sharing anything about his loving mother.

I don't know where these people come from but, they all have their hidden agendas. Christina wanted to replace Stevie with her and the baby, so she went out to sabotage our relationship. She wanted to destroy a relationship just like Renee. I am not going to elaborate on that.

One day, out of the blue, I get a phone call from Renee. She told that she had been thinking about moving to San Antonio where the schools would be better for her two sons. She saw how Stevie's life had improved living with me and she wanted the same for her other sons. She was aware that her youngest son was at risk and wanted to take measures to avoid serious problems. She did not mention this to me but, Stevie had shared it with me before.

I was opened to the idea of her and the boys moving to San Antonio and told her we would need to communicate more in order to make it happen. After that conversation, I never heard from her again.

About a month and a half later Stevie called, and I told him about Renee's call and how I had not heard From her since. He then informed me that she had gotten back with her boyfriend and had gone on a cruise. Once again, she showed a pattern of apathy concerning me as a human being. she could have been decent enough to let me know that she had reunited with her boyfriend and the welfare of her sons was no longer on her list. She just left me hanging to think whatever I wanted to think. That's how Selfish she was. Sure enough her selfishness backfired like it had so many times before. I am so glad she never followed up and they had moved to San Antonio! What a blessing in disguise!

I was infuriated at how she had dismissed me. This would be for the very last time. I wrote her a letter telling her about all the things I had overlooked from the time I met her and that I was not overlooking anything anymore. She thought my heart was made of Teflon and I could handle all her crap. I should have turned my car around when I first got to Paterson and found out she was pregnant. That was only beginning of my journey to Hell. I made it abundantly clear that I was done with her.

A week later Renee called me asking if I was all right. She told me she had received my letter and it sound like a suicide letter. I told her I would never take my life over someone like her. I will never forget how the tone in her voice changed when she said, "So that's how it is?" She then hung up the phone.

Next, I received a call from Stevie asking me what I had done to his mom. He said she had called him crying about some letter I had sent her. The contents of the letter were between Renee and me. Stevie did not have anything to do with it. I asked him if she had shared the contents of the letter with him. He replied that she did not, but he was upset anyway. Although he was well aware of the situation which created the letter, he chose to defend his mother's wrong. He and his mother were of the same mindset. What was he doing ever living in my home? I told him that nothing Good had come from that marriage. There had been no healthy relationships. We all would have been better off if he had stayed with his crazy wicked mother.

Stevie was waiting for me to make that statement so he could completely cut off all ties with me. Let him tell it, he has never been in San Antonio in his life. I wish that had been true. As much as I had wanted to have a healthy relationship with my son it was not meant to be. Since my father had been absent in my life, I wanted to make it better for him. Now, I must re-think my position. I have not heard or seen my son in over twenty-two years. He has totally forgotten who saved him from his mother's wicked insanity. If he were to come to my home, I would not let him in. If I had known then what I know now, I would have hung up the phone when his mother asked for help. What difference would it make.

All attempts to have a relationship with him have been in vain. For the rest of his life he will walk this earth with my blood running through his veins and celebrate his birth on my birthday. Often he had tried to hurt me by saying my wife left me for another man. That never had an impact on me. What he really needed to recognize was how his true love, Denice rejected him because her parents wanted better for their daughter. His living in the projects with a crazy mother did not make him a good candidate to be in their daughter's life. It would have been nice if there had been more parents like them in this story.

Was Sylvia Renee mentally unstable or just another evil spirit? Many of her behaviors indicate some degree of mental illness. However, the choices she made were her evil, willful, intent. My strongest memory of her will be her living conditions at Park Avenue. This represented that we reap what we sow.

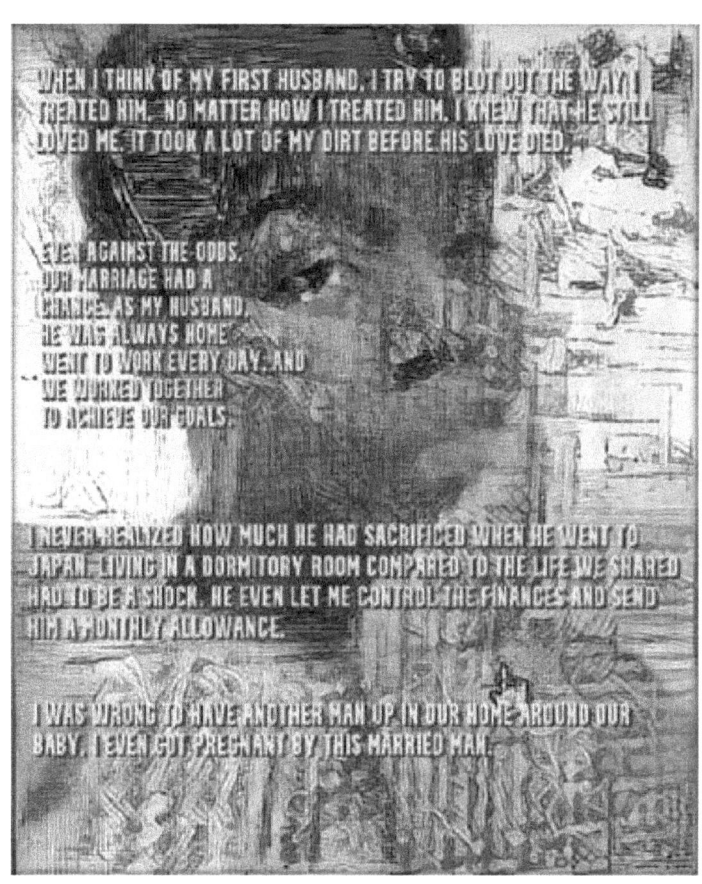

WHEN I THINK OF MY FIRST HUSBAND, I TRY TO BLOT OUT THE WAY I TREATED HIM. NO MATTER HOW I TREATED HIM, I KNEW THAT HE STILL LOVED ME. IT TOOK A LOT OF MY DIRT BEFORE HIS LOVE DIED.

EVEN AGAINST THE ODDS, OUR MARRIAGE HAD A CHANCE. AS MY HUSBAND, HE WAS ALWAYS HOME, WENT TO WORK EVERY DAY, AND WE WORKED TOGETHER TO ACHIEVE OUR GOALS.

I NEVER REALIZED HOW MUCH HE HAD SACRIFICED WHEN HE WENT TO JAPAN. LIVING IN A DORMITORY ROOM COMPARED TO THE LIFE WE SHARED HAD TO BE A SHOCK. HE EVEN LET ME CONTROL THE FINANCES AND SEND HIM A MONTHLY ALLOWANCE.

I WAS WRONG TO HAVE ANOTHER MAN UP IN OUR HOME AROUND OUR BABY. I EVEN GOT PREGNANT BY THIS MARRIED MAN.

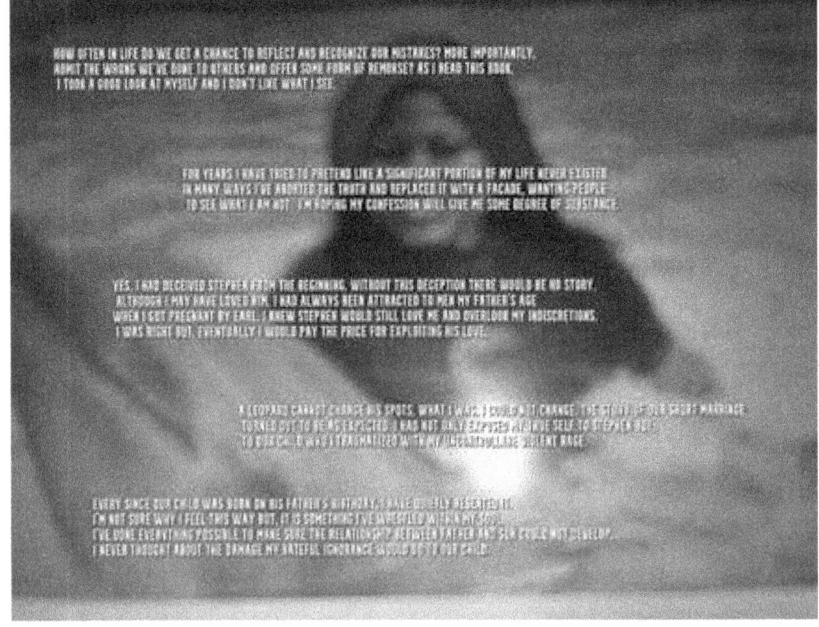

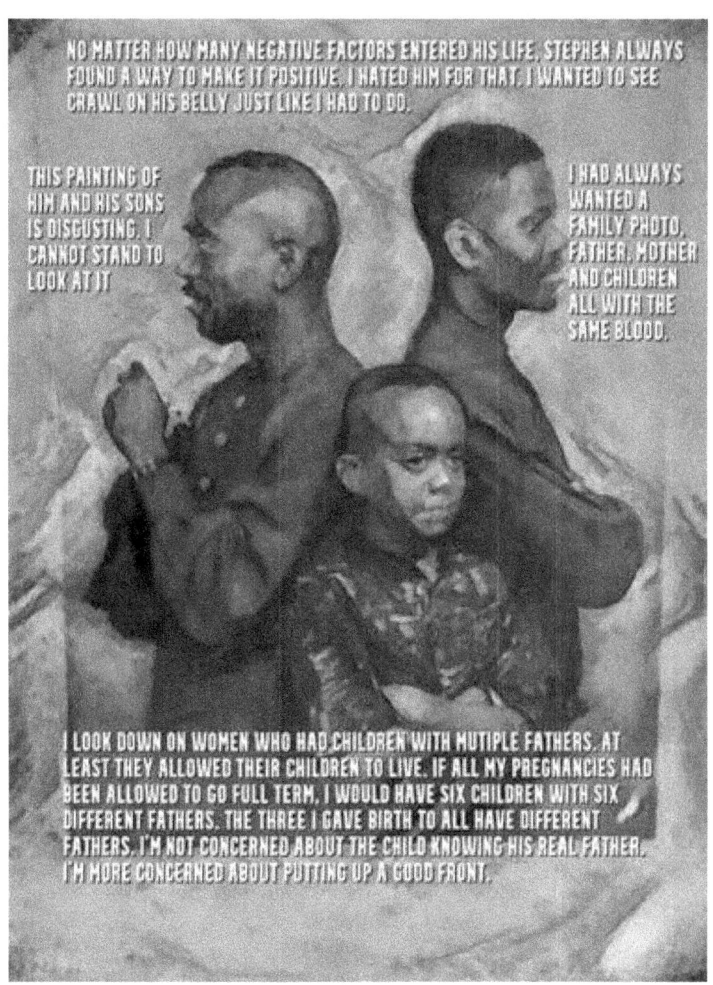

AFTER ALL THE DIRT I GAVE TO STEPHEN, I COULD STILL DEPEND ON HIM. WHO ELSE WOULD HAVE TAKEN ME AND MY KIDS TO DISNEYWORLD? LOOK WHAT I GAVE HIM IN RETURN. EVEN HIS OWN SON WANTED HIM OUT OF THE ROOM WE HAD PAID FOR. IT'S UNDERSTANDABLE HOW HE WOULD WANT TO MOVE ON.

HOWEVER, WHEN I FOUND OUT THAT HE GOT MARRIED, PURCHASED A NEW HOUSE, AND HAD A NEW SON, I WAS INCENSED. JUST BECAUSE WE HAD TREATED HIM SO BADLY WAS NO REASON FOR HIM TO SEEK A NEW LIFE.

I HAD ALWAYS USED OUR SON TO PUNISH HIM. NOW THAT HE HAD A NEW SON, IT WAS TIME TO EMPLOY A DIFFERENT STRATEGY. I ADVOCATED FOR OUR SON TO BE A PART OF STEPHEN'S LIFE. I SENT HIM TO VISIT KNOWING HE WOULD BE MY AGENT OF HATE. I KNEW STEPHEN WOULD NEVER REJECT OUR CHILD. THIS WAS MY OPENING TO FURTHER INFILTRATE HIS LIFE. HE AND HIS WIFE WERE LIVING LIKE KINGS AND QUEENS WHILE WE WERE BARELY SURVIVING. EVEN THOUGH I HAD REMARRIED, IT HAD NOT IMPROVED MY CONDITIONS.

I FELT THAT HIS LIFE WAS MY HOUSE. AFTER ALL THE DIRT I DID, HOW COULD I THINK I DESERVED ANYTHING FROM THIS MAN? HE HAS SHOWED HIS LOVE EVER AFTER OUR DIVORCE, AND I ONLY TOOK ADVANTAGE OF IT.

TO TELL THE TRUTH, HE WOULD HAVE BEEN BETTER OFF LEAVING ME AND ANYTHING THAT WAS CONNECTED WITH ME. COMPLETELY OUT OF HIS LIFE. I WAS NOT GOING TO LET HIM ENJOY IT.

SOMETHING THAT OUR SON NEVER DISCLOSED IS BEING WITH HIS FATHER. THIS WAS A GOOD THING FOR HIM SINCE HIS FATHER WAS THE BETTER PARENT. EACH TIME OUR SON SPENT TIME OR LIVED IN MY HOME, AND ON ONE OF COURSE BECAUSE HIS FATHER'S LIFE.

I MUST ADMIT THAT LIVING WITH HIS FATHER WAS A GOOD THING FOR OUR CHILD. HE GRADUATED FROM HIGH SCHOOL, A THING HE NEVER LISTED AT THE MY PLACE. ALTHOUGH I HAVE NOT STATED, I WAS VERY PLEASED HOW HE HAD HELPED OUR SON.

THE PREVIOUS WHILE HE WAS STEPHEN'S HOME. SEPTEMBER, 1998. HE AND HIS NEW WIFE ALSO OFFERED MARRIAGE AND STEPHEN FELT IT WAS BEST. HE ASSUMED CUSTODY OF THEM TWO. HE HAD BECOME A FOSTER PARENT OF BOTH HIS KIDS. I WAS WORLDS APART FROM OUR CAMPAIGN BACK FATHER. I WAS SO HAPPY FOR HIM.

TWO YEARS LATER OUR SON WAS DISCHARGED FOR FAILURE TO ADAPT. OF COURSE, I BLAMED STEPHEN FOR ALLOWING HIS CHILD IN THE ARMY IN THE FIRST PLACE.

RECOGNIZING THAT A FIVE DAY STEPHEN HAD GIVEN OUR SON, I CALLED AND SUGGESTED THAT HIS FATHER'S WOULD BE A GOOD PLACE TO HAVE HIM ONCE TWO DAYS. STEPHEN WAS OPEN TO THE IDEA AND AGREED FOR MORE COMMUNICATION. I CAN ONLY TELL HIM THAT BECAUSE I WAS SCARED OF BEING BY MY SON. ONCE THE TWO GOT BACK TOGETHER, I SIMPLY PUSHED THE DINNER IDEA AND NEVER PUT IT IN PLACE.

I HAS GOTTEN FOR SO LETTERS STEPHEN SENT MY GRAND OF PLACE. HE HAD TO FIND OUT CHANGED OUR SON. STEPHEN WROTE ME A LETTER STATING HE WOULD NO LONGER OVERLOOK ALL OF MY BAD. HE TOLD ME ONCE A WEEK. IT WAS AT THAT POINT THAT I CALLED OUR SON STATING OF THE DANGER. LETTER HIS FATHER HAD SENT ME. EVEN THOUGH I KNEW I WAS WRONG, I KNEW IT WOULD PERSUADE OUR SON TO CUT OFF COMMUNICATION WITH HIS FATHER. HE HAS NOT SEEN OR TALKED WITH HIS FATHER IN OVER TWENTY-FIVE YEARS.

THIS LATE-LIFE DEBACLE HAS RESULTED IN THE WORLD OF THIS BOY.

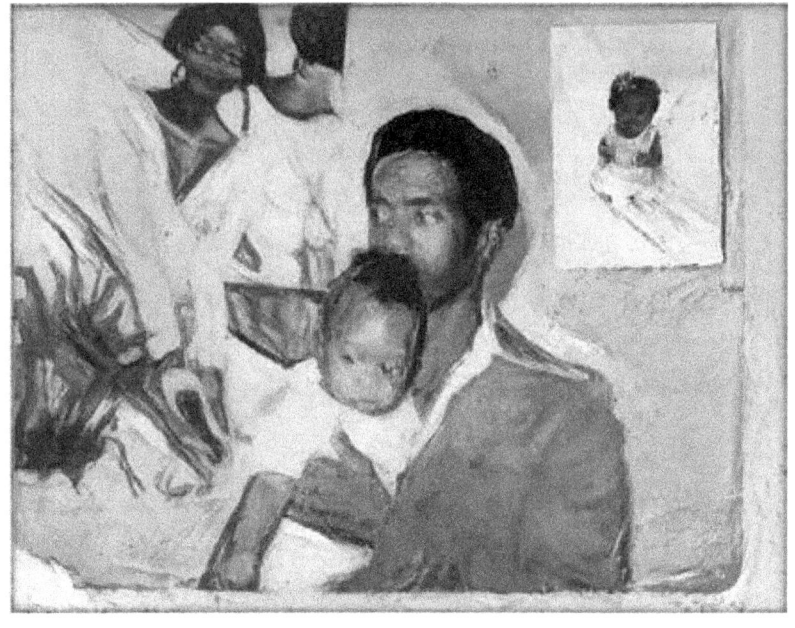

www.ingramcontent.com/pod-product-compliance
Lightning Source LLC
Chambersburg PA
CBHW061739070526
44585CB00024B/2734